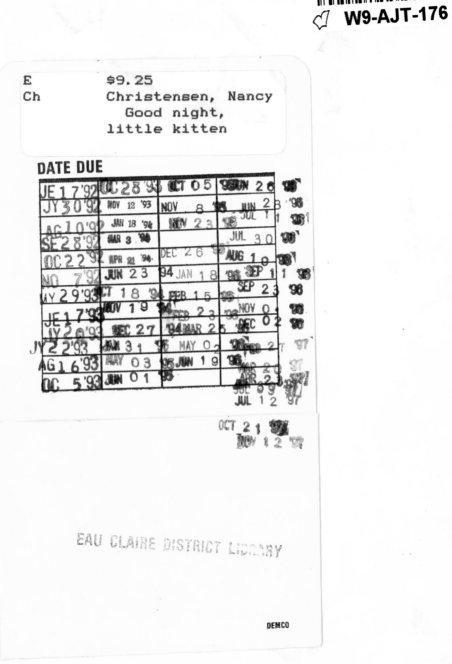

Good Night, Little Kitten

Note

Once a reader can recognize and identify the 24 words used to tell this story, he or she will be able to read successfully the entire book. These 24 words are repeated throughout the story, so that young readers will be able to easily recognize the words and understand their meaning.

The 24 words used in this book are:

and	good	must	stay
bed	I	night	time
but	it's	now	to
don't	kitten	Papa	up
for	little	said	want
go	Mama	sleep	you

Library of Congress Cataloging-in-Publication Data
Christensen, Nancy.
    Good night, little kitten/by Nancy Christensen: illustrated by Dennis Hockerman.
      p. cm — (My first reader)
    Summary: A reluctant little kitten resists his parents' attempts to get him to go to bed.
    ISBN 0-516-05354-X
      (1. Bedtime — Fiction. 2. Cats — Fiction.) I. Hockerman, Dennis, ill. II. Title. III. Series.
PZ7.C45264Go 1990
(E) — dc20

90-30156
CIP
AC

Good Night, Little Kitten

Written by Nancy Christensen   Illustrated by Dennis Hockerman

ℚ CHILDRENS PRESS ®

CHICAGO

Text © 1990 Nancy Hall, Inc. Illustrations © Dennis Hockerman.
All rights reserved. Published by Childrens Press®, Inc.
Printed in the United States of America. Published simultaneously in Canada.
Developed by Nancy Hall, Inc. Designed by Antler & Baldwin Design Group.

1 2 3 4 5 6 7 8 9 10 R 99 98 97 96 95 94 93 92 91

"Good night, Little Kitten,"

said Mama.

"I don't want to go to sleep,"

said Little Kitten.

"You must go to sleep,"

said Mama.

"I want to stay up,"

said Little Kitten.

13

"Good night, Little Kitten,"

said Papa.

"But I don't want to go

to sleep," said Little Kitten.

"It's time for bed,"

said Papa.

"I want to stay up,"

said Little Kitten.

"Go to sleep now!"

said Mama and Papa.

"Little Kitten...

"Little Kitten...

"Good night, Little Kitten!"